LINCOLNWOOD PUBLIC LIBRARY
W9-CDX-420

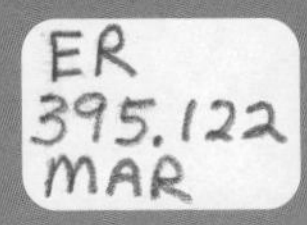

KIDS CAN MAKE MANNERS COUNT

PLEASE AND THANK YOU

3

by Katie Marsico

Cherry Lake Publishing • Ann Arbor, Michigan

Published in the United States of America
by Cherry Lake Publishing
Ann Arbor, Michigan
www.cherrylakepublishing.com

Content Adviser: Tonia Bock, PhD, Associate Professor of Psychology,
University of St. Thomas, St. Paul, Minnesota

Photo Credits: Cover and pages 1, 4, 6, 8, 10, 14, 16, and 20,
©Denise Mondloch; page 12, ©Arkady Mazor/Shutterstock, Inc.;
page 18, ©Vetal/Shutterstock, Inc.

Library of Congress Cataloging-in-Publication Data
Marsico, Katie, 1980–
Please and thank you! / by Katie Marsico.
p. cm.—(Kids can make manners count) (21st century basic skills library)
Includes bibliographical references and index.
ISBN 978-1-61080-433-2 (lib. bdg.)—ISBN 978-1-61080-520-9 (e-book)—
ISBN 978-1-61080-607-7 (pbk.)
1. Etiquette for children and teenagers—Juvenile literature. I. Title.
BJ1631.M335 2013
395.1'22—dc23 2012001703

Cherry Lake Publishing would like to acknowledge
the work of The Partnership for 21st Century Skills.
Please visit *www.21stcenturyskills.org* for more information.

Printed in the United States of America
Corporate Graphics Inc.
July 2012
CLFA11

TABLE OF CONTENTS

Trouble over a Treat

Mark was visiting his Aunt Sally. She was baking chocolate cupcakes.

He was very hungry.

"I want a cupcake," said Mark. He took one of the cupcakes.

Mark stared at Aunt Sally
when he finished eating.

Then he reached for another
cupcake!

Aunt Sally was not happy with
Mark's **manners**.

Making Manners Work

Mark liked visiting his aunt.
He loved her cupcakes.

Yet sometimes he forgot
to be **polite**.

Aunt Sally had a few ideas
about good manners.

She talked to Mark about saying please and thank you.

They are **important** ways to show good manners.

THE UNITED STATES OF AMERICA
FEDERAL RESERVE NOTE
THIS NOTE IS LEGAL TENDER
FOR ALL DEBTS, PUBLIC AND PRIVATE
F
F 91553386 D
WASHINGTON, D.C.
WASHINGTON
ONE DOLLAR
SERIES
2003
A
Secretary of the Treasury.
B 43
6
1

Mark thought about times when he said please and thank you.

He said please when he asked his parents for lunch money.

He said thank you after they gave it to him.

Practicing Please and Thank You

Aunt Sally thought Mark should always **practice** good manners.

Did he want food at a friend's home? She told him to say please before asking.

Maybe someone shared food with Mark. Aunt Sally told him to say thank you.

They talked about other ways to use these important words.

Mark began saying please if
he wanted to borrow a toy.

He started saying thank you
if someone gave him a gift.

Soon Mark was saying please and thank you all the time.

Aunt Sally liked his good manners.

Mark still enjoyed her cup-cakes. He always told his aunt please and thank you!

Find Out More

BOOK

Brown, Marc. *D. W. Says Please and Thank You*. New York: Little, Brown, 2011.

WEB SITE

Whyzz—Why Do I Have to Say Please and Thank You?
www.whyzz.com/why-do-i-have-to-say-please-and-thank-you
Learn more about the importance of these words, as well as how to say them in other languages!

Glossary

important (im-POR-tuhnt) powerful or valuable

manners (MA-nurz) behavior that is kind and polite

polite (puh-LYT) being well behaved, using good manners

practice (PRAK-tis) to do something regularly

Home and School Connection

Use this list of words from the book to help your child become a better reader. Word games and writing activities can help beginning readers reinforce literacy skills.

a
about
after
all
always
and
another
are
asked
asking
at
aunt
baking
be
before
began
borrow
chocolate
cupcake
cupcakes
did
eating
enjoyed
few
finished
food
for
forgot
friend's
gave
gift
good
had
happy
he
her
him
his
home
hungry
I
ideas
if
important
it
liked
loved
lunch
making
manners
Mark
Mark's
maybe
money
not
of
one
other
over
parents
please
polite
practice
practicing
reached
said
Sally
say
saying
shared
she
should
show
someone
sometimes
soon
stared
started
still
talked
thank
the
then
these
they
thought
time
times
to
told
took
toy
treat
trouble
use
very
visiting
want
wanted
was
ways
when
with
words
work
yet
you

Index

About the Author

Katie Marsico is an author of children's and young-adult reference books. She lives outside of Chicago, Illinois, with her husband and children.